AMERICAN HOLIDAYS

★ ★

Election Day

Heather C. Hudak

Weigl Publishers Inc.

Published by Weigl Publishers Inc.
350 5th Avenue, Suite 3304
New York, NY 10118-0069
Website: www.weigl.com

Library of Congress Cataloging-in-Publication Data

Hudak, Heather C., 1975-
  Election day / Heather C. Hudak.
      p. cm. -- (American holidays)
  Includes index.
  ISBN 1-59036-404-X (hard cover : alk. paper) -- ISBN 1-59036-407-4 (soft cover : alk. paper)
  1. Election Day--Juvenile literature. 2. Elections--United States--Juvenile literature. I. Title. II. American holidays (New York, N.Y.)
  JK1978.H83 2007
  324.973--dc22
                                            2005029035

Printed in the United States of America
1 2 3 4 5 6 7 8 9 0 10 09 08 07 06

Editor Heather C. Hudak
Design and Layout Terry Paulhus

Cover Many Americans exercise their right to vote on Election Day. They vote to choose the leaders of their city, state, and country.

Contents

Introduction

DiD YOU KNOW?

Each presidential term lasts four years. Presidents can hold office for a maximum of two terms, or eight years.

Election Day is the day after the first Monday in November each year. On this day, any of the states can hold an election. People vote in elections for leaders. These leaders are called public officials. Countries where people vote are called democracies.

People running for president must be at least 35 years of age and citizens of the United States. They must also have lived in the country for at least 14 years.

On Election Day, most Americans 18 years of age or older can vote. Every four years on Election Day, people vote for electors. They are representatives of the 50 states. Electors cast their votes for the **president** of the United States.

4

Political conventions, or gatherings, are an important part of the election process in
the United States. Many Americans go to these conventions to show support

Election History

George Washington was the first president of the United States.

The United States declared **independence** from Great Britain on July 4, 1776. Each state was given the power to make voting and election laws.

On January 7, 1789, the first presidential election took place. George Washington was the first president of the United States. John Adams became the first vice-president.

At first, only landowners were allowed to vote. By 1860, all men of European background over the age of 21 were allowed to vote. After the **American Civil War**, men of all **ethnic** backgrounds were able to vote. Then, in August of 1920, a law was passed granting women the right to vote in federal elections.

DID YOU KNOW?

Only 3 percent of Americans were given the right to vote between 1789 and 1860. Sixteen presidents were elected during this time.

George Washington took the Oath of Office at Federal Hall in New York City. Federal Hall was the first capitol of the United States.

The Election Process

Most Americans do not vote for the president.

Before Americans can vote, they must register with their district. To register, voters fill out a form that provides information about their identity. People can usually register by mail.

Most Americans do not vote for the president. On Election Day, they vote for an elector, who supports the person they want to be president. This is called the popular vote. It is held in November.

The Electoral College votes for the president every four years in December. The college is made up of electors representing the 50 states. Their vote makes the popular vote official. The new president is declared on January 6 and is sworn into office on January 20. This day is called Inauguration Day.

DID YOU KNOW?

The Electoral College has chosen the president and vice-president of the United States since 1789.

8

Presidential campaigns begin months before Election Day. Candidates travel around the country, make speeches, and greet voters.

The Electoral College casts the official votes for the president and vice-president of the United States 41 days after Election Day.

Election Day

Not all districts use the same method of voting.

On Election Day, Americans vote at polls. Polls are usually public buildings, such as a schools, recreation centers, or firehouses. Not all districts use the same method of voting. Some use devices, such as voting machines or computers. Others have paper ballots.

Once all votes are in, poll workers count the ballots. Election officials tally votes around the state and around the nation. The **president-elect** with the most votes wins.

★ ★ ★ ★ ★ ★ ★ ★ ★ ★
At the close of an election, all ballot boxes are taken to a single location for tallying. The results are declared shortly after.

Election Day 2000

The presidential election in 2000 was one of the closest elections in United States history. Voters went to the polls on November 7. The presidential candidates were George W. Bush and Al Gore. They both received many popular votes. The votes for each person were very close in many states. Some places had to count the votes twice. Five weeks passed before there was a winner. It was the longest election in more than 100 years.

George W. Bush represented the Republican Party, while Al Gore represented the Democratic Party.

Creating the Holiday

★ ★

Election Day is a legal holiday in 27 states.

In 1845, the United States **Congress** decided to make Election Day a November holiday. It chose the day after the first Monday in November.

Election Day is a legal holiday in 27 states. In these states, citizens are given a day off school and work. The government is working on a bill to make Election Day a holiday in every state. It would be called Democracy Day.

★ ★ ★ ★ ★ ★ ★ ★ ★

Americans vote for candidates in the House of Representatives and the Senate. These two houses make up the United States Congress.

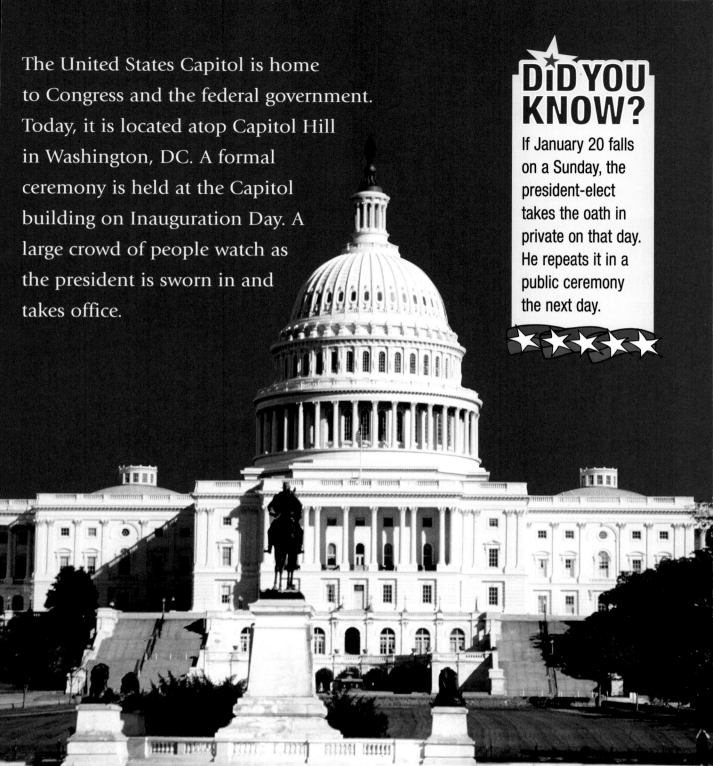

The United States Capitol is home to Congress and the federal government. Today, it is located atop Capitol Hill in Washington, DC. A formal ceremony is held at the Capitol building on Inauguration Day. A large crowd of people watch as the president is sworn in and takes office.

At noon on January 20, the new president takes the Oath of Office on the steps of the United States Capitol.

Celebrating Today

★ ★

Television, radio, newspapers, and the Internet bring election news to people across the United States and around the world.

Today, many people run for office. They must compete for support. Presidential candidates make television commercials. They tour the country and hold conventions. Large crowds of people in cities and towns gather at these conventions. Candidates give speeches to gain support from electors and voters.

Television, radio, newspapers, and the Internet bring election news to people across the United States and around the world. This helps people learn about candidates and what they believe in.

★ ★ ★ ★ ★ ★ ★ ★ ★

The presidential election is televised in countries around the world, including Korea, Germany, Pakistan, Egypt, and Russia.

Holding a political convention requires a great deal of equipment, including television lights, speakers, fog machines, confetti, and balloons.

America Votes

Americans have the right and the privilege to vote. It is important to be part of the process. Voting allows people to voice their opinions. There are many voting systems. Here are just a few of the systems used across the United States.

In Oregon, most people vote using an optical scan system. This is a system where voters use a pen to color a symbol beside the name of the person they are voting for. Then, voters place the ballot in a computer. The computer reads the symbol. It tallies the total votes.

Oregon

Nevada

In 1985, Nevada voters began using a mechanical voting system. This system allows voters to pull the lever of the candidate they wish to elect. This system was first used in New York in 1892.

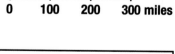

0   100   200   300 miles

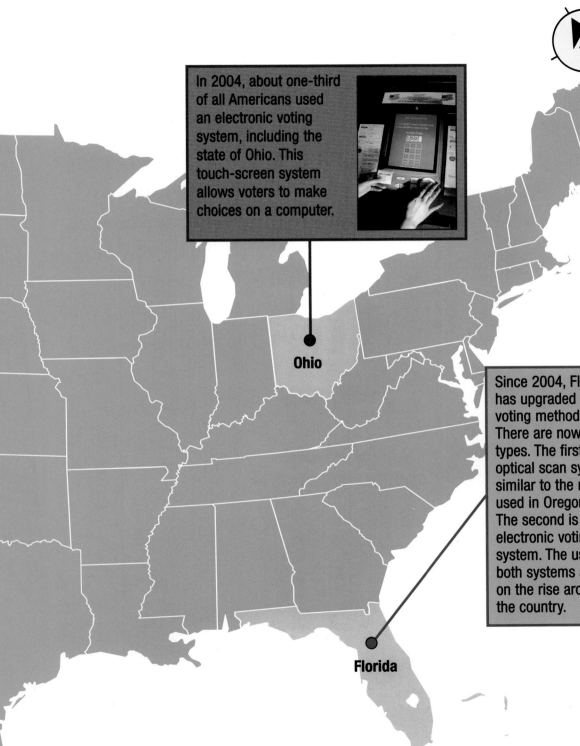

In 2004, about one-third of all Americans used an electronic voting system, including the state of Ohio. This touch-screen system allows voters to make choices on a computer.

Ohio

Since 2004, Florida has upgraded its voting methods. There are now two types. The first is an optical scan system similar to the method used in Oregon. The second is an electronic voting system. The use of both systems are on the rise around the country.

Florida

Holiday Symbols

Election Day is an important time in the United States. Each election is a part of America's history. There are many symbols that are part of Election Day history and events.

★ ★ ★ ★ ★ ★ ★ ★ ★ ★

The bell tower atop Independence Hall once housed the Liberty Bell. The bell symbolized freedom in the United States.

Independence Hall

Independence Hall was built between 1732 and 1756. It is located in Philadelphia, Pennsylvania. The **Founding Fathers** wrote the **Declaration of Independence** at Independence Hall in 1776. The American flag was designed there in 1777. The **Constitution** of the United States of America was written there the following year.

The Oath of Office

Every public official must say an oath of office. The oath is a promise to uphold the constitution. The president-elect must take the oath at noon on January 20 of the year the term begins. The president-elect makes the promise in front of thousands of Americans.

The Constitution

In 1787, the Founding Fathers wrote the Constitution of the United States of America. The Constitution is made up of laws. It also tells how the government should work. The Constitution took effect in 1789 and has been a model for laws of other countries around the world. The original copy of the Constitution is found in the National Archives in Washington, DC.

Further Research

Many books and websites explain the history and traditions of Election Day. These resources can help you learn more.

Websites

To find out about election processes, symbols, and the government, visit:
http://bensguide.gpo.gov

To learn more about the White House and the presidents of the United States, visit:
www.whitehouse.gov/kids

Books

Catrow, David. *We the Kids*. New Jersey: Dial Publishing, 2002.

Gottfried, Ted. *The 2000 Election*. Connecticut: Millbrook Press, 2002.

Crafts and Recipes

Lunch Menu Election

In class, form four groups. Each group chooses a snack food they would like to place on a lunch menu. The groups then urge others to vote for their food. Each group can decorate a ballot box and design ballots. On the ballot, mark an X beside the food you wish to vote for. Then place your ballot in a ballot box. Select two students to count the ballots. The two students then declare a winner.

Who Is Leading?

Use the Internet to find presidential Election Day results from the past. Next, photocopy a black and white map of the United States. Choose a crayon color for each candidate. Use

Al Gore   George W. Bush

these crayons to color each state where the candidates won the popular vote. For example, in 2000 George W. Bush ran against Al Gore. Color each state Gore won blue. Then, color each state Bush won red. Be sure to include a legend. It should show which color represents each candidate.

Election Day Recipe

Banana Split

Ingredients:
2 scoops of vanilla ice cream
1 ripe banana
strawberries, blueberries
blue and red sprinkles

Equipment:
ice cream scoop, oval deep
dish or banana boat

1. Ask an adult to slice the banana in half lengthwise. Place at bottom of dish.
2. Place 2 scoops of vanilla side by side on top of the banana.
3. Sprinkle washed strawberries and blueberries around the dish.
4. Top the scoops of ice cream with blue and red sprinkles and serve.

Election Day Quiz

What have you learned about Election Day? See if you can answer the following questions. Check your answers on the next page.

1 When is Election Day?

2 Who votes for the American president?

3 Who wrote the Constitution of the United States of America?

4 Name three Election Day symbols.

5 Who was the first president of the United States?

President Abraham Lincoln was the first Republican president. The Lincoln Memorial in Washington, DC, was dedicated to him in 1922.

Fascinating Facts

★ In 2004, 47 percent of 18 to 24 year olds voted. Sixty-six percent of Americans age 25 or older voted, too.

★ There are 538 electoral votes in a presidential election. To become president, a candidate must receive 270 votes.

★ In the United States, most public officials belong to one of two main political parties. These parties are called the Democratic Party and the Republican Party.

★ Americans have elected 41 different presidents in 53 elections. All have been men. Most have served the country as public officials, vice presidents, or military leaders.

Quiz Answers:
1. Election Day is on the day after the first Monday in November.
2. Electors vote for the American president.
3. The Founding Fathers wrote the Constitution of the United States of America.
4. Three Election Day symbols are the Constitution, the Oath of Office, and Independence Hall.
5. George Washington was the first president of the United States.

Glossary

American Civil War: military conflict between the northern and southern states from 1861 to 1865

Congress: the national government body of the United States

constitution: a written document containing the basic laws of a nation

Declaration of Independence: a written document declaring the United States' freedom from Great Britain

ethnic: having to do with a group of people with distinctive cultural traits

Founding Fathers: members of the group that wrote the constitution

independence: having the ability to support oneself

president: the leader of the United States government

president-elect: a person who is running for president

Index